Essential Lives

FIDEL CASTRO

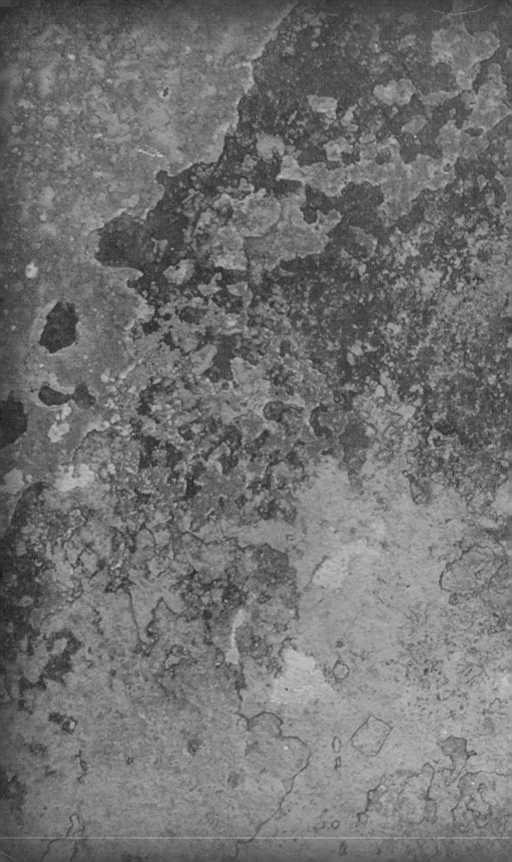

FIDEL CASTRO

CUBAN PRESIDENT & REVOLUTIONARY

by Katie Marsico

Content Consultants:
David Cingranelli, PhD, and Therese Cingranelli, MS
Department of Political Science, Binghamton University

ABDO
Publishing Company

CREDITS

Published by ABDO Publishing Company, 8000 West 78th Street, Edina, Minnesota 55439. Copyright © 2009 by Abdo Consulting Group, Inc. International copyrights reserved in all countries. No part of this book may be reproduced in any form without written permission from the publisher. The Essential Library™ is a trademark and logo of ABDO Publishing Company.

Printed in the United States.

Editor: Rebecca Rowell
Copy Editor: Paula Lewis
Interior Design and Production: Emily Love
Cover Design: Emily Love

Library of Congress Cataloging-in-Publication Data
Marsico, Katie, 1980-
 Fidel Castro : Cuban president & revolutionary / by Katie Marsico.
   p. cm. — (Essential lives)
 Includes bibliographical references and index.
 ISBN 978-1-60453-522-8
 1. Castro, Fidel, 1926—Juvenile literature. 2. Cuba—History—1959-1990—Juvenile literature. 3. Heads of state—Cuba—Biography—Juvenile literature. 4. Revolutionaries—Cuba—Biography—Juvenile literature. [1. Castro, Fidel, 1926- 2. Heads of state. 3. Cuba—History—1959-] I. Title.
 F1788.22.C3M258 2009
 972.9106'4092—dc22
 [B]
                                    2008033493

TABLE OF CONTENTS

Fidel Castro began fighting for his beloved country as a young man.

A POWERFUL PROMISE

idel Castro trudged through the muck
of a Cuban mangrove swamp in late
1956. Occasionally, he paused to shout words of
encouragement to the 82 men who trekked with
him. The 30-year-old revolutionary was as weary as

his followers, but he was also relieved to be back on his native shores. Castro's homecoming followed more than a year in Mexico. There, he organized and trained rebel forces to overthrow Cuban dictator Fulgencio Batista before being thrown out of the country.

Cuba had long been the site of violent political unrest and abusive, oppressive government leaders. Castro was not pleased with Batista's leadership and wanted change. The young guerrilla commander had plotted to displace Batista a few years before, but his attack on the Moncada Barracks in July 1953 had failed miserably. The interim provided time for Castro to organize and train his followers in guerrilla tactics. This time, Castro planned to defeat Batista after arriving in southeastern Cuba on December 2, 1956.

Castro and his soldiers had learned from experience that winning back their country would involve danger, discomfort, and risk. On this particular expedition, the men had endured a rough ocean voyage across the Gulf of Mexico

Castro's Ferocious Spirit

Batista was aware of Castro's ferocious spirit. A few weeks before his return from Mexico, Castro issued this statement to the dictator in a pro-government newspaper: "We strongly reaffirm the promise we made for the year 1956: We will be free men or martyrs."[1]

The Power of Attitude

Castro knew that his band of rebels was vastly outnumbered by more than 30,000 of Batista's soldiers in late 1956. In his mind, success lay far more in attitude than in numbers. Castro later recalled, "I began a revolution with 82 men. If I had do it again, I'd do it with 10 or 15 and absolute faith. It does not matter how small you are if you have faith and a plan of action."[3]

and the Caribbean Sea. They lacked sufficient supplies, and the trip lasted five days longer than anticipated. Finally on Cuban soil, the hungry and thirsty rebels prowled through muddy terrain knowing that Batista's forces were most likely aware of their presence.

Castro could do little to relieve his troops as they headed toward the dense rain forest of the Sierra Maestra Mountains, except to possibly recall the noble reason for their suffering. Such an opportunity arose when the group stumbled upon a peasant. Castro quickly reassured the surprised man by laying his hand on the man's shoulder and explaining to him:

> I am Fidel Castro. My companions and I have come to liberate Cuba. You have nothing to fear from us because we have come to help the peasants. We shall give them land to work, markets for their products, schools for their children and decent housing for the whole family.[2]

This would not be the last time Castro would speak this powerful promise. Time would soon

Upon returning to Cuba, Castro and his troops headed toward the Sierra Maestra Mountains to battle Batista and his troops.

reveal that Castro was destined to play many roles, including daring revolutionary, heroic liberator, controversial leader, and despised tyrant.

Defining an Island's Identity

Much has happened to Castro since the rebel leader made his way across ocean waters to return home to fight for his country. He has become recognized worldwide as much more than a government resister. Castro shaped a nation that remained at the forefront of news headlines while under his control. Some herald him as the genius behind a renowned revolution that brought positive change and political recognition to Cuba. Others label him as a bully and longtime threat to international peace and security.

The undisputed leader of Cuba for nearly five decades, Castro's name is forever intertwined with the country's identity. Claiming to desire a better life for his people—particularly the underclass—he instituted communist policies that granted him ultimate control over politics and the economy. Without the rebel leader, the small country may not have captured such widespread public attention during the twentieth and twenty-first centuries.

Castro has been the center of debates, intrigue, and warfare. This is the result of his political maneuvers, his temper, and his intolerance for anyone who opposed his authority. In addition

Reaching Cuba

If Castro and his troops had hoped to find relief from their troubled sea voyage as soon as they reached Cuba's shoreline, they were sorely disappointed. Forced to abandon most of their supplies, the men carried their rifles above their heads as they staggered through swamps that reduced their speed and made them easy targets for Batista's soldiers. As Castro's comrade Captain Juan Manuel Márquez sarcastically remarked, "It wasn't a landing, it was a shipwreck."[4]

to introducing a communist state to the Western Hemisphere, Castro has been at the center of damaging trade embargos, a crisis surrounding nuclear weapons, and heated questions related to immigration and refuge for political exiles.

A percentage of Castro's fellow citizens credit him with improving education and health care by ensuring that these resources were not exclusively allocated to wealthy or influential Cubans. In their eyes, Castro freed them from

Castro's Many Faces

While some look upon Castro with awe and admiration, others regard him with deep-rooted resentment and disappointment. For many Cubans, Castro represented several admirable ideals before he became Cuba's leader. However, some critics believe that he allowed his need to exercise complete authority to supersede the best interests of the people.

After fleeing Cuba, Rufo López-Fresquet, Cuba's former minister of the treasury, said the following of Castro:

The Castro who paid generously for the food he received from the peasants, who fed and cared for his prisoners, who founded schools, who submitted his political decisions [for] consideration—the Castro who did all this while he was fighting against the dictatorship—acted as a revolutionary. But after Castro took power, he changed.[5]

According to López-Fresquet, Castro is a talented actor who skillfully interwove charm and intimidation to keep an entire country under his thumb beginning in 1959. "His height, his broad shoulders, his clear diction, and his determined air . . . were indeed impressive. . . . He was the symbol of power, and power always is frightening."[6]

United in Song

Castro and his men departed Mexico in November 1956 in less-than-ideal conditions. Rain was pouring, and their boat was cramped and in need of repair. The future seemed far from certain. But Castro's enthusiasm and the worthy cause of liberating their country helped alleviate some of his men's apprehension. The fighters later recalled that their spirits were bolstered by the stirring words of the Cuban national anthem. The song reinforced the glory of their mission and patriotically promised, "To die for the motherland is to live!"[7]

centuries of uncaring and unjust rule. These loyalists revere him as the reason Cuba has gained international stature—even if the island's politics have not always been viewed in a completely positive light.

Despite conflicting opinions about Castro, few can argue his determination to achieve social justice for the poorest of Cuba's people or his intense and unwavering faith that he had the ability to do just that. ⌐

Castro during a public appearance in April 2006

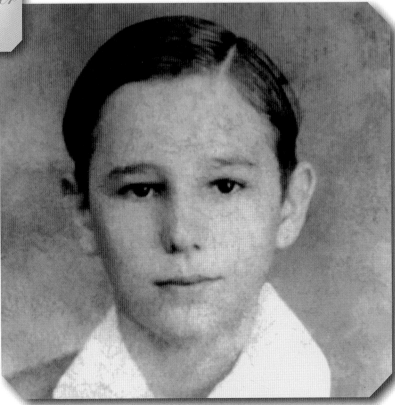

Fidel Castro during his time as a student at La Salle College

Young Fidel

Cuba—formally known as the Republic of Cuba—has a population exceeding 11 million. The small nation is a long, narrow island located 90 miles (145 km) south of the United States. It is bordered by the Atlantic Ocean, the Gulf of Mexico, and the Caribbean Sea. Cuba was primarily inhabited by indigenous people prior to the arrival of explorer Christopher Columbus in 1492. In 1763, Spain exchanged Florida to England in return for Cuba as part of a treaty. When Cuba was acquired by Spain, thousands of indigenous people were killed. Some died of illnesses introduced by the Europeans. Others proved unable to endure the brutal treatment of their conquerors.

Over time, the colony became increasingly recognized as a bountiful source of coffee, tobacco, sugar, and metals such as iron, nickel, gold, and copper. Laborers were needed to work the farmland and mines. Spaniards brought vast numbers of African slaves to Cuba. The mixing of cultures has resulted in residents who have a combination of indigenous, Hispanic, and African roots.

By the 1800s, Cuba's population surpassed 1 million. Beginning in 1860, approximately one-third of the world's sugar supply originated in Cuba. With its prized exports and

Fidel's Awareness

Growing up with the advantages of money, Fidel was aware of the bitterly contrasting existence that the underclass endured. Comparing his own life to the lives of the laborers on his father's plantation, he once noted, "I was born into a family of landowners in comfortable circumstances. . . . Everyone lavished attention on me, flattered [me], and treated me differently from the other boys we played with when we were children. These other children went barefoot while we wore shoes; they were often hungry; at our house, there was always a squabble at the table to get us to eat."[1]

close proximity, U.S. citizens eyed
the area with growing interest.

Islanders wanted independence
from Spain. In 1868, Cubans began
revolting against their Spanish
oppressors. They won independence
from Spain when U.S. troops battled
Spain during the Spanish-American
War in 1898. However, most Cubans
felt far from liberated. U.S. forces
continued to occupy much of Cuba
after the war. In addition, several
native government leaders were
corrupt, brutal, or simply ineffective
at creating lasting positive change.

Young Rebel

Fidel began to cultivate
his abilities as a rebel
leader at an early age.
When Fidel was 13 years
old, he infuriated his father by openly accusing
him of treating his laborers unfairly. Fidel did not
stop there. Although his
efforts did not take root,
he urged the farmhands
to strike.

The United States played an enormous role
in Cuba's economy. U.S. citizens owned a large
percentage of the country's sugar factories and
fueled tourism to the capital city of Havana. U.S.
leaders did not hesitate to dispatch soldiers when
they believed U.S. economic investments were in
jeopardy. For Cubans, the issues at stake were not
simply about money or the United States. Some
Cubans enjoyed financial success because of the
sugar trade. But a larger number wondered when

they would have a decent education, health care, and adequate housing. These Cubans believed the country was in desperate need of change. Decades later, Fidel Castro would be one of these many Cubans.

A Leader Is Born

Fidel Alejandro Castro Ruz was born on August 13, 1926. Fidel's father, Ángel Castro y Argiz, immigrated to Cuba from Spain. He experienced considerable success in Cuba as a sugarcane farmer. His plantation sat nestled in the

Ally or Unwelcome Influence?

In early 1898, the United States sent the battleship USS *Maine* to Havana's harbor to protect U.S. citizens in Cuba during the bloody combat between the Cubans and the Spanish. At that point, U.S. forces were not officially involved in the conflict. But on February 15, a mysterious explosion sank the *Maine* and claimed the lives of more than 260 sailors.

U.S. newspapers fueled suspicions that the Spanish were at fault—often using excited headlines and less-than-truthful reporting. As a result of the intense pressure brought by the media, the Spanish-American War erupted. The United States overthrew Spanish control in portions of Latin America and the western Pacific. Many Cubans were initially delighted by this outcome, but it soon became clear that the United States intended to keep control of Cuba's political and military affairs. Cuba appeared to be independent, but the United States reaffirmed its powerful presence when it opened a naval base at Guantánamo Bay in southeastern Cuba in 1903. U.S. officials also monitored Cuba's economy and its new government. Several Cubans bristled at this ongoing foreign interference. Decades later, Castro would continue to complain about what he perceived as the United States' "great contempt, scorn, and disdain for the Cuban people."[2]

Cuba is located 90 miles (145 km) south of the United States.

foothills of the Cristal Mountains near the village
of Birán.

Fidel was Ángel Castro's third child from
a relationship with his housekeeper, Lina Ruz
González. Following Fidel's birth, the couple
eventually married and had four more children.

Fidel was surrounded by hundreds of workers who labored hard and received little in return for their effort. In contrast, Fidel enjoyed a privileged life. He had the benefit of fine clothes, plentiful food, and a private education.

Around 1933, Fidel's parents sent him to Santiago de Cuba to attend La Salle College, a private Catholic school. Young Fidel initially pined for his home and his mother. But his sadness quickly gave way to his fiery spirit and strong-willed resistance to authority figures who attempted to control him. Fidel once faced expulsion for supposedly striking a teacher who tried to physically discipline him. He later recalled of the incident:

> *It was a decisive moment in my life, . . . I felt that taking me away from school was a punishment I didn't deserve. . . . I told [my mother] . . . that if I wasn't sent back [to school], I'd set fire to the house. . . . I really threatened to set the whole place on fire.*[4]

Contacting the White House

On November 6, 1940, Fidel mailed a three-page letter to President Franklin D. Roosevelt. He told the U.S. leader, "I am a boy, but I think very much. If you like, give me a ten dollars bill green American in the letter because I have not seen a ten dollars bill American, and I would like to have one of them."[3] Fidel never received the ten dollars he requested, but he spoke publicly of his deep respect for Roosevelt in the years to come.

WORTHY OF ESTEEM

Fidel moved on to the Jesuit preparatory boarding school Dolores College in Santiago de Cuba in 1940. In 1942, he enrolled at the Jesuit College of Belén in Havana. Fidel excelled in history and geography. In addition, his determination and intense personality earned the respect of classmates.

Eighteen-year-old Fidel completed his courses at Belén in 1945. By that time, he had revealed his drive to overcome obstacles and his tendency to fearlessly combat those who opposed his will. "I [did not] dream I was preparing to be a guerilla," he admitted years later, "but every time I saw a mountain, it was a challenge to me. The idea of climbing that mountain, of reaching the top, would seize me."[5] This yearning to achieve would become more pronounced with time. ⌐

FIDEL CASTRO RUZ

Castro's 1945 high school yearbook photograph

Students protest at Havana University in 1947. Castro fit in well with the school's political atmosphere.

INTENT ON CHANGE

ollowing his graduation from Belén, Castro began to study law at Havana University in October 1945. Havana University proved the perfect setting for 19-year-old Castro. He slipped into college life with relative ease, quickly becoming a member of the student group Unión Insurreccional Revolucionaria (UIR), or Revolutionary Insurrectional Union.

The UIR was one of a handful of campus groups dedicated to achieving national reform and rebellion against the Cuban government. Its roots were in Birán, a small town where it was customary for people to bear arms and settle conflicts through physical aggression. Members of student groups often carried pistols. They were not above committing murder in a struggle for control of the campus and as a means of furthering their revolutionary messages.

Castro became increasingly engrossed in Latin American politics. By the summer of 1947, he was involved in an unsuccessful attempt to overthrow a violent dictator in the Dominican Republic. Less than a year later, he played a role in organizing a student congress in Bogotá, the capital of Colombia. When Eliécer Gaitán, the liberal opposition to the conservative ruling

Intercepted

Much to Castro's frustration, the Cuban navy intercepted the boat that he and other revolutionaries were using for passage to the Dominican Republic in the summer of 1947. As military personnel transferred the rebels to another vessel and prepared to head back to Havana, Castro leapt overboard into the Bay of Nipe along the northeast coast of Cuba. According to Castro's version of events, he then swam in full uniform through shark-filled waters and walked 20 miles (32 km) to reach Las Mañacas.

party, was shot on April 9, 1948, violence erupted in the streets. Rioters set fires and destroyed property. Castro eagerly participated in the chaos. He later recalled, "I was filled with revolutionary fervor, trying to get as many people as possible to join the revolutionary movement."[1] Several Colombian officials suspected that Castro was responsible for enflaming the riots rather than merely joining them. He scoffed at these accusations. However, he would soon willingly admit to stirring far more monumental unrest in Cuba.

Many Roles

Castro took on many roles as a young man. His reputation as a volatile and sometimes violent revolutionary continued to grow. He also became a husband and a father. On October 12, 1948, he wed Mirta Díaz-Balart, a 22-year-old philosophy student. The couple's only child—Félix Fidel, or "Fidelito"—was born on September 1, 1949. Although he now had a wife and young son, Castro was as consumed as ever by political affairs and had little time for his family.

The Cuban government continued to be defined by corruption and inefficiency. Money always seemed to make its way into the pockets of the elite and powerful. Aristocratic officials delighted in lavish homes and luxuries that peasants, farmers, and laborers could only dream of owning. The Cuban underclass lacked basic education and health care. They toiled doing backbreaking labor that barely afforded them simple necessities.

Bearing these two social groups in mind, Castro insisted that his wife and son live in a humble apartment and resist the urge to take advantage of their families' wealth. He also became increasingly active in the Cuban People's Party, or Ortodoxos. The group pushed for reforms designed to create a more just government structure. Castro was able to balance this commitment with his studies. He graduated in the fall of 1950 with degrees in law, international law, and social science.

Castro was more committed to building his political career than practicing law. He had high

An Unsupportive Father

Castro may have been able to win over struggling laborers and rebellious students as he plotted to overthrow Batista, but the one man he assumed would lend him support remained unimpressed. Castro's father considered his son's proposals to be absurd. He refused to grant Fidel the $3,000 he requested to purchase weapons and ammunition, saying, "It's really stupid to think that you and that starving group of ragamuffins could bring down Batista, with all his tanks, cannons, and airplanes."[2] In the end, he gave Castro $140 with the following farewell: "Have a good trip, you loco [crazy person]. I hope nothing bad happens to you."[3]

A Poor Existence

Although Castro was a lawyer and received a small income from his father, his wife and son were rarely far from living in poverty. Between his political activities and apparent disinterest in using money for anything other than revolutionary causes, Castro proved neglectful of his family's needs. Castro's wife, Mirta, barely had enough money to purchase groceries; her car and pieces of furniture were repossessed. In addition, she and her son lived without power for stretches of time when the electric bill went unpaid.

hopes for the elections of June 1952. His goal was to win a seat in the Cuban House of Representatives. Several of his countrymen saw remarkable potential in the 25-year-old and believed congress would be the foundation of his political career.

Castro's aspirations for the House of Representatives did not survive past spring. On March 10, 1952, one of the presidential candidates organized a coup and rocketed to power. General Fulgencio Batista abruptly seized authority and ordered his soldiers to overtake media channels in Havana. Cuban President Carlos Prío Socarrás fled to Mexico.

MISFORTUNE AT THE MONCADA BARRACKS

Castro was appalled by Batista's declaration of leadership. Batista had served as president from 1940 to 1944 and had been highly influential in government and military affairs prior to that term in office. His political involvement had been considered beneficial to islanders. Batista had

Fulgencio Batista was an influential military leader in Cuba before serving his first term as president from 1940 to 1944. He returned to power in 1952 following a coup.

improved education, public works, and the nation's finances. But the coup in 1952 brought a change in Batista's policies. He was obsessed with obtaining wealth and opened Havana to gambling, casinos, and hotels. Batista was also a harsh ruler. He arrested those who opposed him and strictly controlled the government, press, and public opinion.

Democracy was all but dead in Cuba. Castro was enraged by his people's acceptance of an official he viewed as a despicable tyrant.

Castro challenged Batista in any way he could. He rallied Ortodoxos against Batista, and brought arguments to Cuba's Supreme Court that Batista's coup was unconstitutional. He marched with whatever followers he could find. Castro recruited a greater number of these "Fidelistas," as well as weapons and money. He made plans to win back Cuba with force. His primary strategy was a siege at Batista's Moncada military barracks in Santiago. Castro planned to conquer the fortress and capture its weapons with approximately 160 rebels. Once success was his,

A Charming Leader

Castro's success in rallying anti-Batista supporters is undeniably linked to his immense confidence, spirit, and ability to rouse patriotic pride in his countrymen. A Cuban exile who once was a political prisoner under Castro later commented, "He can mesmerize and charm you and make you his admirer, if not his follower."[4]

Castro sought as followers Cubans who would be open to his message of revolution. While he was indisputably a risk taker, he nonetheless had to exercise caution because Batista showed little mercy to anyone who dared to question his authority, let alone schemed to destroy it. Castro later recalled of the movement to overthrow Batista:

I met a lot of earnest young people . . . in the lowest-income sectors . . . among the workers. We organized that movement in just fourteen months, and it came to have 1,200 men. I talked to every one of them and organized every cell, every group. . . . How many times have I met with future fighters, shared my ideas with them, and [given] them instructions![5]

Castro intended to broadcast news of his victory from the barracks' radio station. He believed his glorious revolution would engulf the entire island. Castro imagined that the countless men and women who were beginning to comprehend Batista's true nature would assist in bringing down his dictatorship.

Some of Castro's comrades hesitated when they heard how he aimed to overthrow approximately 700 government soldiers with considerably fewer troops and a crude collection of weapons. Castro proceeded with his surprise attack. On July 24, 1953, he and a handful of Fidelistas departed Havana and traveled 600 miles (966 km) to Santiago. The rebel commander calculated that his ambush would come at a local fiesta time, when many of the men at the barracks would be exhausted from drinking and celebrating. Bolstered by his enormous self-confidence and his belief in the spirit of the Cuban people, Castro readied for Moncada in the early morning of July 26.

Riding in a convoy of 26 U.S. limousines, Castro and a portion of his forces headed toward the fortress. Unfortunately, some of the drivers had limited knowledge of Santiago's streets and

Abundant Confidence

Famous for both his sizable ego and his considerable fearlessness when it came to political revolution, Castro appeared to have every confidence that he would triumph at the Moncada Barracks. On the other hand, if the attack was not a success, he had rationalized that it would at least have "symbolic and heroic value."[7]

became lost. Castro's brother Raúl was deployed to invade the nearby Palace of Justice. Another portion of the troops was ordered to take control of a local hospital and barracks farther west. The group that arrived at Moncada with Fidel Castro disastrously mistook a barbershop for the armory they had hoped to loot. Mass chaos ensued. Batista's military opened fire on the revolutionaries, killing eight and prompting their leader's retreat into the Sierra Maestra Mountains.

Fidelistas captured by Batista's soldiers suffered greatly. Prisoners were routinely tortured and executed. Castro's self-described legion of "honest, determined young people who had patriotic, progressive ideas" was temporarily left scarred and scattered.[6]

Fidel Castro as a young man

The Model Prison on the Isle of Pines

PRISONER, EXILE, LEADER

ess than a week after the failed attack on
the Moncada Barracks, Batista's troops
discovered Castro asleep in a hut in the Sierra
Maestra. He was taken prisoner on August 1, 1953,
and he faced trial in Santiago for his attempted

revolution. The 26-year-old rebel had made a considerable name for himself in Cuba's political scene.

As Castro's reputation and popularity pushed to greater heights, Batista's oppressiveness also grew in intensity. In the wake of Moncada, it was critical that Batista appear more in control than ever before, so he suspended the constitution and set forth a policy of heavy-handed censorship of the press. Any discussion that appeared to remotely contradict Batista's regime merited harassment, time in jail, or worse.

Castro was not easily intimidated. Representing himself in court, he argued with interrogators and boldly voiced his belief in the righteousness and patriotism of his actions. He fearlessly charged the court, "Sentence me. I don't mind. History will absolve [forgive] me."[1] Castro's judges remained unmoved by his arguments. In mid-October 1953, they sentenced Castro to 15 years in prison. He would serve the time at

José Martí

From an early age, Castro was deeply impressed and inspired by Cuban national hero José Martí, an honored leader of his country's battle for independence from Spain beginning in 1895. As Castro departed for Mexico in July 1955, he voiced support for the forceful and inevitably bloody revolutionary methods that the rebel had put into play 60 years earlier. "Like Martí, I think the time has come to seize our rights instead of asking for them," he asserted. "To grab instead of beg for them. Cuban patience has its limits."[2]

the Model Prison on the Isle of Pines, which is separated from the Cuban mainland by the Gulf of Batabanó.

Prison Life

Castro made the most of his life behind bars. Initially, he had his own stove and was permitted to receive gifts of food and the cigars he so famously enjoyed. In an attempt to pass his sentence as constructively as possible, he devoted himself to reading. He read for 14 to 15 hours a day, including the literary masterpieces of authors such as Dostoevsky, Hugo, and Balzac. Castro also wrote numerous manifestos and letters in invisible ink. In addition, he organized a makeshift school for the other inmates and lectured on topics such as philosophy and world history.

Despite these achievements, imprisonment was clearly not always pleasant. Castro's marriage deteriorated during his time in prison and ended with divorce in early 1955. In addition, Castro was

Isles of Pines Prisoners

In February 1954, prisoners on the Isle of Pines had an unexpected visitor. Batista traveled to the island to dedicate a new power plant that was within close proximity of the inmates. Castro and his followers could not resist an opportunity to voice their distaste for the dictator and chanted their anthem. Batista initially thought the chorus of voices was raised in his honor, but his pleasure quickly turned to fury when he heard the men sing of the "insatiable tyrants who have plunged Cuba into evil."[3]

sometimes kept in solitary confinement because he had been too outspoken or had incited unrest among the other inmates. During such periods, he had limited access to light and little means of learning what was going on in the outside world.

In November 1954, Batista held public elections in an effort to fulfill an earlier promise to do so and to display that his rule was the will of the people. These elections were essentially staged. Batista and his regime bullied any potential opposition until it no longer posed a threat. Perhaps feeling more secure in his position, Batista announced

History Will Absolve Me

While serving his sentence at Model Prison, Castro began taking steps to publish his thoughts on the revolution. Though his pamphlet failed to reach widespread audiences until 1959, *History Will Absolve Me* reflects many of the sentiments Castro expressed during his trial. It also includes his vision for his countrymen. He wrote of reformation of land rights, improved benefits for laborers, and a return to Cuba's earlier constitution, which addressed the need for minimum-wage requirements and public education.

In *History Will Absolve Me*, Castro also described his intended audience and explained how its members possessed the necessary qualities to make his revolution a reality:

When we speak of the people . . . we mean [those] who yearn for a better, more dignified, and more just nation. People, who, to attain these changes, are ready to give even the very last breath of their lives. . . . These are the people . . . who know misfortune and, therefore, are capable of fighting with limitless courage![4]

the release of numerous political prisoners in spring 1955. Castro's sentence came to an early end on May 6.

POLITICAL EXILE

The decision to release Castro from prison may have been Batista's greatest mistake. Upon his release, Castro was discouraged to discover Ortodoxos's unwillingness to back his plans to forcibly remove Batista from power. Equally as frustrating was his inability to use media outlets or to rally any substantial support without commanding unwanted attention from Batista's men. Perceiving the impossibility of further progress from a base in his homeland, Castro headed to exile in Mexico City, Mexico, on July 7, 1955.

In a show of reverence to the Fidelistas who had perished as part of the offensive on July 26, 1953, Castro began referring to his continued political activism as Movimiento 26 de Julio, or the 26th of July Movement. While in Mexico, Castro and the members of his movement prepared to reclaim Cuba. They would have to confront Batista's men with fighters united in their aspirations for Cuba and their loyalty to the revolution. Fidelistas such as

Raúl Castro and a young Argentinean doctor named Ernesto "Che" Guevara eagerly lived up to such ideals.

Members of the 26th of July Movement readied themselves for a revolution by studying the art of guerrilla warfare. It was crucial for them to make devastating surprise attacks on the Cuban army. The men learned how to hide from enemies and then hit them hard. They also planned to harass Batista's camps and patrols to drive his men into a state of chaos and surrender. During this time, Castro relied on the generosity of others to support his movement and the training of his men. Castro traveled extensively to raise funds for weapons and supplies. In October 1955, he visited the United States to seek out the kindness of wealthy Cuban exiles willing to support him and his cause.

As Castro and his men prepared to fight Batista's army, Mexican

Meeting Guevara

Castro met 27-year-old Che Guevara in the summer of 1955. Unknowingly, he was shaking hands with a man who would be instrumental in helping him win and maintain power. The Argentinean intensely admired Castro's ferocity of spirit and unwavering belief in his ability to reclaim Cuba. This respect was reciprocated by Castro, who expressed the following sentiments after the rebel commander's death in 1967: "Che was an incomparable soldier. . . . [He] carried to its highest expression . . . the revolutionary spirit of sacrifice, revolutionary combativeness, [and] the revolutionary's spirit of work."[5]

Spared

While many of the Fidel-
istas who attacked the
Moncada Barracks faced
torture and execution,
Castro was spared by one
of Batista's lieutenants.
When Pedro Sarría found
the rebel in the Sierra
Maestra, Castro quietly
urged Sarría not to reveal
his identity to the military
patrol. Realizing how
bloodthirsty the dictator's
soldiers were in the wake
of the attack on July 26,
Sarría reasoned that Cas-
tro had a better chance
of survival if he was not
immediately disclosed as
the leader of the attack.

Castro never forgot Sar-
ría's good will and even
promoted him to the rank
of captain after assuming
power. Castro later said
of Sarría, "Unquestion-
ably, that man—one in a
thousand—sympathized
in some way with . . . our
cause. He was really re-
sponsible for our survival
at that moment."[6]

officials became less tolerant of
the rebels. Castro and most of his
followers had tourist passes, and the
government was not eager to openly
serve as the training ground for
political radicals. Mexican police
began seizing Castro's weapons
and insisting that the Cubans find
another place to train.

Castro bought a sea-battered yacht
named the *Granma.* In the early hours
of November 25, 1956, he and 82
of his troops set sail from Tuxpan,
Mexico, for a turbulent journey
home. They were going to take back
Cuba.

Castro and his troops traveled from Tuxpan, Mexico, to Cuba in late November 1956.

Castro's followers included women. Here, Castro poses with nurses who work for his rebel army, the 26th of July Movement.

¡Viva Fidel!

astro's journey home from Mexico was less than ideal. His men suffered aboard the *Granma*, gripped by seasickness in the crowded and unreliable vessel. Castro had planned to make landfall within two days of his departure.

At this time, comrades already in Cuba would be participating in scheduled revolts. However, Castro and his rebels arrived on December 2, 1956—two days late. Castro and his crew did not have enough supplies during their crossing. The men were hungry and thirsty as they struggled through a mangrove swamp on their way to the Sierra Maestra.

Batista's soldiers were aware of the rebels and harassed them with planes and artillery fire. Batista's soldiers used loudspeakers to tempt the rebels with the promise that they would be dealt with decently if they surrendered. On December 5, the revolutionaries suffered a handful of casualties and were temporarily scattered after encountering enemy troops. The rebels were forced to flee into the hills. The Castro brothers, Guevara, and fewer than 20 of the original fighters regrouped over the course of the month. Many of their companions had been captured and executed.

Batista made certain that the media reported Castro's demise and

Surviving on Sugarcane

Famished, parched, and disastrously short on supplies, Castro and some of his men made use of Cuba's vast sugarcane fields shortly after their homecoming in December 1956. They cut the raw stalks, sucked out the sweet inner juices, and tossed any chewed segments to the ground. Unfortunately, this left an easy trail for Batista's troops, who closely studied the bits of gnawed stem and tracked the rebels' progress toward the mountains.

Castro and his followers used whatever resources they could find, and even built some equipment, including this armored vehicle.

the success of his own men. By December 13, 1956, he declared that Castro's rebels had been overcome and there was no need for his own army to canvass the area. Batista's confidence did little to increase his popularity. Castro's message had spread, and riots and violent protests became commonplace in major cities such as Havana. Citizens were weary of an economy that seemed to benefit only upper-class associates favored by Batista. The dictator had little patience for such grumbling. He imprisoned, tortured, or murdered anyone who opposed him.

As tension mounted across the island, Castro and his supporters grappled with the unfamiliar terrain of the Sierra Maestra. Batista's army faced the equally frustrating challenge of locating the rebels in the thick vegetation and hidden passes. Political sympathizers aided the revolutionaries by smuggling supplies to them and gradually adding to their ranks. Castro was encouraged by this support and the people's growing hatred for Batista. This encouragement, and his developing talent for strategy, helped Castro generate a series of attacks on military garrisons in the Sierra Maestra beginning in January 1957. He used these raids to steal ammunition and other necessities. The raids were also opportunities for Castro's men to fine-tune their skills as guerrillas.

Fighting Batista

Although Castro began launching successful attacks against Batista's military in 1957, he wanted government soldiers to know that he hated Batista, not them. Castro was acquainted with José Quevedo Pérez, the major who had been sent to stamp out the rebel forces in the summer of 1958. "It was difficult to imagine when you and I knew each other at the university, that someday we would be fighting each other," Castro wrote shortly after the officer's arrival. "Even so, perhaps we do not harbor different feelings about our fatherland."[1]

Fighting a Losing Battle

Within weeks, Castro started the next phase of his attack by launching a media assault on Batista. Castro realized that many Cubans believed he was dead because of Batista's manipulation of the press. Castro organized interviews with international journalists who subsequently assured the world of his ongoing dedication to the revolution. After meeting Castro in February 1957, *New York Times* reporter Herbert Matthews wrote, "President Fulgencio Batista . . . [is] fighting a

---

The Role of Reporters in the Revolution

Castro realized that it was not sufficient for visiting journalists to simply report that he had survived Batista's offensive after arriving in Cuba. In order to muster greater support, Castro needed to demonstrate that he had the means to vanquish much larger government forces. As a result, he prepared a bit of a show for *New York Times* reporter Herbert Matthews in February 1957. He ordered his troops to bathe, clean their rifles, and practice marching in military formation. They could not afford to appear as a collection of filthy ruffians who were scouring the mountains in search of food and the occasional enemy garrison to attack.

Castro also staged interruptions during the interview, arranging for his men to deliver crucial-sounding messages about military affairs. He discussed his visions for Cuba and explained the numerous improvements he would impart to the people. Following the interview, Castro confidently issued a public message that challenged government control of the media: "Can Batista go on hiding from the country and the whole world what is happening here? The interview we had in the heart of the Sierra with [the] *New York Times* correspondent will be published . . . any minute now."[2]

losing battle to destroy the most dangerous enemy [he] has yet faced."[3]

Time proved this assessment accurate. Castro continued to gain followers. He kept up attacks on enemy troops stationed in the mountains. With 30,000 to 40,000 men, Batista's army was at least four times the size of the 26th of July Movement. But Castro was convinced that strength lay in more than numbers. Batista's military was ineffectively organized, and his soldiers undoubtedly found it difficult to be completely devoted to their ruthless commander. Other countries began shying away from his horrific brutality. The United States withdrew military assistance in spring 1958.

Batista was relentless against Castro. In summer 1958, he sent 10,000 men into the Sierra Maestra to put an end to Castro and his attacks. Castro was prepared for the affront; his guerrillas had acquired superior combat skills. The mountains were peppered with supporters who shared Castro's ideals and kept him informed of the movements of Batista's army. In addition, most of Cuba was attuned to Castro's achievements. He frequently communicated with comrades outside the region using a radio transmitter. By the end of July 1958, Batista's

Castro's Appearance

A reporter offered the following description of Castro shortly after his rise to power: "What he wears is not some smart parade-ground gear, but crumpled olive-green battle-dress. His shirt is open at the collar. . . . His face is a little bloated, but [he] has a healthy color. His shaggy, matted beard makes the long dark-brown cigars almost disappear between his bulging lips. He has a way of lazily eying his surroundings [that] expresses complete self-confidence, and [that has] a hypnotic power you are unable to escape. . . . Castro's deep voice is husky, but also cracked—which may be precisely why it captivates many of those who hear it."[4]

offensive had all but crumbled. The soldiers he sent were either ambushed or had surrendered. Castro decided it was the ideal time to spread his liberation to the streets of Havana.

Castro ordered some of his fighters to head west and a second group to head to the center of the island. He led a third segment toward Santiago. By fall 1958, it was obvious that Batista was incapable of stopping the revolution. Fearing for his life, he relinquished control of Cuba and fled to the Dominican Republic before the sun rose on January 1, 1959. Castro arrived in Havana about a week later.

THE WORLD REACTS

Castro was greeted in Havana by throngs of citizens celebrating and shouting, "Viva Fidel!"[5] The mood was jubilant, and the sight of flags and armbands bearing the insignia of the 26th of July Movement seemed to promise only positive change. But Cubans—and the world—could not help but wonder what such change would entail.

Castro quickly took steps to reaffirm his refusal to repeat Batista's mistakes. He was adamant that he would not officially head the new government. He advocated the presidency of Manuel Urrutia Lleó, the judge who pardoned Castro in 1957 on the grounds that rebellion against dictatorship was not a crime. The president was sworn in on January 3, 1959. Castro would serve as commander in chief and do his part to "launch an offensive against corruption, immorality, gambling, stealing, illiteracy, disease, hunger, exploitation, and injustice."[6]

The rest of the world did not rejoice in Castro's goal as readily as the Cubans. U.S. leaders were especially on edge. They had not been pleased with Batista's tyrannical policies, but they were wary of the potential consequences of a guerrilla rebel rising to power. Their apprehension was compounded by fears surrounding Castro's views on communism. In its ideal form, communism refers to a communal, or shared, economic and political system based on the principle "from each according to their

Castro, right, talks with President Manuel Urrutia, center, in January 1959.

ability to each according to their need."[7] It stresses that the control of the productive enterprises in a society should be owned by the workers whose labor is essential to the production process. In a true communist state, social classes cease to exist, government is unnecessary, and everyone lives in abundance. However, no modern government has come close to achieving the communist ideal.

Today, the term *communism* refers to authoritarian or undemocratic political systems in which private ownership of property is forbidden or extremely limited. Communist leaders such as Castro claim to advance the rights of the masses, peasants, and workers. However, citizens and workers have few, if any, ways to influence government policies. Such communist philosophies are directly opposed to the combination of democracy and capitalism favored in the United States.

Castro's opinions on social and economic ideologies were critical to U.S. leaders who were already entangled in an ongoing conflict with another communist nation, the Soviet Union. The Soviet Union had been embroiled in bloodless discord with the United States since the end of World War II. The two countries were considered superpowers, and

No Foreign Interference

Castro adamantly proclaimed that his revolution would bear one striking difference to the political upheaval with Spain in 1898. Unlike that struggle, the triumph of 1959 would not be tainted by foreign interference. "The revolution begins now," he declared to an excited crowd in Santiago on January 2, 1959. "This time, luckily for Cuba, the Revolution will truly come into power. It will not be like 1898, when the North Americans came and made themselves masters of our country. . . . [T]his time, it will really be the Revolution. . . . I am sure . . . that for the first time, the republic will be entirely free."[8]

each superpower pushed for a firmer grasp on world domination. Each country scrambled to outdo the other's advances in everything from space exploration to military technology to industrial productivity. By 1959, no actual combat had defined what had become known as the Cold War. There was no guarantee the situation would not change if communism took root in Cuba. ⌐

Fidel Castro addresses a crowd gathered in the park in front of the presidential palace in Havana, Cuba, in January 1959.

Fidel Castro and Nikita Khrushchev embrace at the United Nations General Assembly in New York, New York, on September 20, 1960.

Maximum Leader

astro's first year as commander in chief of Cuba was challenging. Almost immediately, his intention to overshadow Urrutia's role as head of the government became apparent. But the people did not seem to mind. They loved

Castro and listened with admiration to his long, impassioned speeches about the need for education and economic reform.

Castro was becoming an expert politician and pressured prominent officials who disagreed with his opinions to resign. On February 16, 1959, he was appointed prime minister after the man who held that office lost patience with Castro's overbearing interference and quit. About this time, Castro was proclaimed Cuba's "Maximum Leader."[1]

A majority of U.S. citizens were impressed by Castro when he visited the United States in April 1959. Castro assured the nation that his political agenda did not involve communism. President Dwight D. Eisenhower and Vice President Richard Nixon remained unconvinced. Officials began to contemplate the likelihood of future U.S. efforts to remove Castro from power.

Back in Cuba, Urrutia and other politicians also questioned

Opposing Castro

Even Castro's closest associates had no guarantee of how he would react if they openly opposed his opinions. In late October 1959, a commander named Huber Matos was arrested on treason charges after he resigned because of his dissatisfaction with communist influence within the revolution. Raúl Castro wanted Matos shot. By the end of the year, Matos was found guilty and began serving a 20-year prison sentence. Once released, he fled Castro's regime and took up residence with his family in Costa Rica and then the United States.

Castro's true intentions. He introduced measures
that forced wealthy plantation owners to sacrifice
their land in exchange for bonds. Their property
was given to peasants and members of the Cuban
underclass. In addition, the government took
control of major businesses such as telephone and
telegraph companies. Some of these corporations
were owned by foreign interests, which added to U.S.
apprehension.

Castro's authority seemed to increasingly override
any laws or government structures that did not
suit him. He interfered in the trials of accused war
criminals who had served Batista. Castro rejected a
sentence that acquitted 43 members of the air force.
He then demanded a new hearing that concluded
with the guilty verdicts he obviously desired. He held
power, and the free elections he had mentioned in
early 1959 appeared not to be forthcoming.

Enemies and Allies

Castro won the loyalty of the masses. This
caused friction between Castro and Urrutia. In
July 1959, the pair butted heads when Urrutia
publicly expressed his distaste for communism. In
response, Castro abruptly resigned as prime minister

during a television broadcast on July 17. "I am not a communist," Castro announced, "but we do not have to say we are anticommunists just to curry favor with foreign governments."[2] Regardless of his political preferences, the people were in an uproar over Castro's decision. They cried for the return of their hero. Already stripped of much of his power, the president was manipulated into giving up what remained of it by Castro's actions. By July 26, Castro resumed the responsibilities of prime minister, and Urrutia fled Cuba. Communist lawyer Osvaldo Dorticós Torrado was named president. Raúl Castro was appointed minister of defense.

Castro was adored by many, especially peasants and laborers. But the middle and upper classes were concerned with his authority. Wealthy plantation owners rejected his drastic steps toward land redistribution.

Agrarian Reform Act

On May 17, 1959, Castro signed the Agrarian Reform Act into law. This legislative measure essentially removed farmlands spanning more than 1,000 acres (405 ha) from the control of their owners and redistributed the property among approximately 200,000 peasant families. Castro had the following words for the men and women who were losing rights to their land in exchange for bonds: "Great landowners must understand that their duty is to adapt themselves to the new circumstances....Nobody feeling like a Cuban, no real patriot, can fail to understand that this . . . will be of benefit to the nation."[3]

Men and women with university degrees and successful professional careers bristled at the thought of a communist regime that denied them democratic elections. From their perspective, Castro's strides toward providing more widespread public education and free medical care were overshadowed by other aspects of his government.

These citizens were disturbed by Castro's increasing control of the press and disregard for viewpoints other than his own. Castro showed no hesitation in imprisoning or intimidating

Contrasting Perspectives

Nikita Khrushchev expressed great enthusiasm for Castro. When he and Castro appeared before the United Nations General Assembly in September 1960, he demonstrated indisputable support for Castro's rant against the United States. Journalist Hans Ulrich Kempski described how Khrushchev frequently—and noisily—expressed his adoration "like that of a fan at a football match who has lost all restraint."[4]

To the contrary, Kennedy's condemnation of Castro was readily apparent before he was elected president of the United States. The young politician noted at a political dinner on October 6, 1960:

Castro and his gang have betrayed the ideals of the Cuban revolution and the hopes of the Cuban people. . . . [He] is not just another Latin American dictator—a petty tyrant bent merely on personal power and gain. His ambitions extend far beyond his own shores. He has transformed the island of Cuba into a hostile and militant communist satellite. . . . [The United States] can hardly close its eyes to a potential enemy missile or submarine base only 90 miles from our shores.[5]

those he perceived as threats to his revolution. Not
perceiving enough distinctions between Castro and
Batista, and continuing to be alarmed by Castro's
communist tendencies, such islanders started
emigrating to Miami, Florida. Creating their own
"Little Havana" in that city, they nonetheless had
no desire to be away from their homeland for long.
Several of these Cubans plotted to overthrow Castro,
and U.S. officials were not going to stop them.

Infuriated by the exiles and the U.S. support
for them, Castro cultivated his friendship with the
Soviets. In February 1960, he and Soviet Premier
Nikita Khrushchev developed a controversial trade
agreement that guaranteed the Soviet Union's
purchase of 504,000 tons (457,221 t) of sugar
from the Cubans throughout 1960, then 1 million
tons (907,185 t) a year for the next four years.
The Soviets also promised to provide Castro with
necessities such as oil and grain. U.S. oil companies
refused to allow their Cuban refineries to be
involved in the processing of oil distributed by their
Cold War enemy. In response, Castro seized U.S.-
owned companies such as Texaco, Esso, and Shell.
He then similarly nationalized other U.S. industries
and properties. This action ultimately cost U.S.

citizens billions of dollars in foreign investments.

Eisenhower dealt with Castro's actions by increasing trade restrictions. First, he cut 700,000 tons (635,000 t) of sugar imports from the island in the summer of 1960. Next, he eliminated all exports to Cuba in October. Eisenhower authorized the Central Intelligence Agency (CIA) to train Cuban exiles to invade their homeland and effectively remove Castro from power. Some of these Cubans had already flown out of Florida and dropped bombs and anti-Castro leaflets onto Cuban soil. However, they had never before received such active encouragement of their anti-Castro activities from the U.S. government.

Castro believed he was protected. He had been openly assured by Khrushchev that he would have Soviet military support if threatened. When President John F. Kennedy took

Soviet Help

Khrushchev was not shy about his willingness to extend Soviet friendship to the people of Cuba as the Soviet Union and the United States grew increasingly bitter toward one another. When Eisenhower increased U.S. trade restrictions with the island, Khrushchev quickly interjected that his nation would purchase the 700,000 tons (635,036 t) of sugar that the United States refused to buy in July 1960. Perhaps most disturbing to U.S. officials was a speech Khrushchev made that same month, in which he said, "One should not forget that now the United States is no longer at an unreasonable distance from the Soviet Union. . . . Should the need arise, Soviet artillerymen can support the Cuban people by missile fire."[6]

the oath of office in January 1961, the likelihood of
bloodshed on Cuba seemed greater than ever.

THE BAY OF PIGS

Relations between Castro and Kennedy were
rocky from the start. The popular young U.S.
politician based a portion of his election campaign
on the previous administration's inability to
subdue Castro. Shortly before Eisenhower's term
as president ended, the United States had formally
ended all diplomatic interactions with Cuba. Not
long after Kennedy took the oath of office, the new
president authorized the CIA to progress with its
training of Cuban exiles for an intended invasion of
Cuba. But the attack did not go as planned.

Air strikes were scheduled to destroy Castro's
fighter planes on April 15, 1961. But the first of
these assaults failed to do sufficient damage, and
Kennedy did not order the second assault. The
landing force of the 1,511 exiles at the Bay of Pigs
along southern Cuba was to occur following the
air strikes. When the exiles arrived two days later,
on April 17, 1961, they were met with artillery fire
from Castro's pilots and 20,000 ground troops. By
April 19, the invasion had failed: 1,189 of the Cuban

Castro, lower right, sits inside a tank during the Bay of Pigs invasion, on April 17, 1961.

invaders went to prison, 114 had been killed or drowned, and only a few had escaped.

CUBAN MISSILE CRISIS

As Castro savored his victory, he grew bolder in his maneuvers with the Soviet Union. He formally declared his revolution to be socialist, and he and Khrushchev agreed to place medium-range nuclear missiles on the island the following July. In mid-October 1962, U.S. anxieties escalated when a U.S. spy plane took photographs of the warheads. Kennedy recognized that the proximity of these weapons to his country threatened the lives of countless U.S. citizens.

During this time, Kennedy and Khrushchev engaged in a series of threats, ultimatums, and denials. This became known as the Cuban Missile Crisis. Kennedy instituted a naval blockade of Cuba, declaring that Soviet ships traveling within 500 miles (805 km) of the island would be subject to attack. He also warned Khrushchev that any missile launched from Cuba would warrant a decisive U.S. military response.

As the two superpowers moved dangerously close to igniting a nuclear war, Castro controlled the nation at the center of the dispute. The global community focused on

Operation Mongoose

On November 30, 1961, Kennedy authorized the CIA to move ahead with Operation Mongoose, a secret undertaking to overthrow Cuba's government. Several of the plans involved assassination attempts on Castro or activities that would undermine his authority as leader. One plot was rooted in the theory that the loss of his famous beard would diminish his aura of power. Operatives from the "dirty tricks" division were responsible for odd, fanciful ideas to overthrow Castro. They suggested that dusting Castro's clothing with toxic powders would do the trick, as the chemicals would cause his facial hair to fall out.

Cuba. In a speech broadcast on television and radio on October 23, 1962, Castro confidently assessed:

> *All of us, men and women, young and old, we are all united in this hour of danger, and ours, the fate of all the revolutionaries and the patriots, will be the same fate, and the victory will belong to all.*[7] ‿

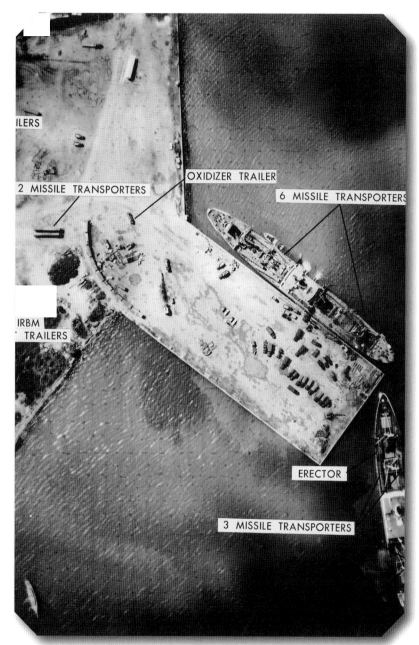

ILERS

2 MISSILE TRANSPORTERS

OXIDIZER TRAILER

6 MISSILE TRANSPORTERS

IRBM
TRAILERS

ERECTOR

3 MISSILE TRANSPORTERS

*This photograph shows Soviet missile equipment being loaded at the
Mariel naval port in Cuba on November 5, 1962.*

Fidel Castro, left, clasps hands with Nikita Khrushchev atop the Lenin mausoleum in Moscow's Red Square on May 1, 1963.

STRUGGLING TO SURVIVE

By late October 1962, the world's attention was focused on Cuba. Tensions during the Cuban Missile Crisis reached a high point when Soviet vessels bound for Cuban shores approached the U.S. naval blockade on

October 24. Much to Kennedy's satisfaction, the
Soviet ships reduced their speed and ultimately
reversed their course before coming
within 500 miles (805 km) of the
island. Four days later, the crisis
ended when Khrushchev announced
that he planned to remove all nuclear
warheads from Cuba.

Khrushchev and Kennedy came
to an agreement that resulted in
the removal of Soviet weapons from
Cuba and a guarantee that the United
States would not invade the island
nation. Kennedy also promised to
eliminate U.S. missiles positioned
in Turkey, which posed a threat
to the Soviet Union. Much of the
global community was relieved by
the compromise, but Castro was
anything but pleased. He was insulted
by not being included in any of the
negotiations between Kennedy and
Khrushchev. Castro had been eager
to demonstrate that Cuba was capable
of standing on its own.

Angered by the Soviet Response

Although Castro did not
sever diplomatic relations
with the Soviet Union,
he was enraged at that
nation's resolution of the
Cuban Missile Crisis. He
was particularly angered
by the fact that he had
not been called upon to
participate in any nego-
tiations. In early 1963,
Castro was quoted as
saying that "he would box
[Khrushchev's] ears" if the
Soviet leader ever visited
the island.[1] Castro later
echoed the reasons for his
fury, explaining, "I would
have taken a harder line
than Khrushchev. I was
furious when he compro-
mised."[2]

Castro's Initiatives

In the early 1960s, Castro facilitated several initiatives to help his country and his people. Some of his plans were well received. For example, he declared 1961 the "Year of Education" and sent some 300,000 literate Cubans into rural areas to teach approximately 700,000 local peasants to read. He also worked to ensure that all Cuban citizens had employment, adequate housing, and free health care.

However, other aspects of Castro's regime proved less appealing. The economy in his new communist state suffered as a result of a U.S. trade embargo. When Kennedy banned tourism to the island in February 1963, Cubans lost another valuable source of revenue. Cubans also suffered when Castro modified the country's proven agricultural system. He wanted Cuba to rely less on trade and reduce economic dependence

Worthy of Victory

Castro knew what was at stake as the Cuban Missile Crisis intensified. He later indicated that any bloodshed by his countrymen would have been well worth the reward of defeating the United States. In a letter to Khrushchev on October 31, 1962, Castro wrote, "Few times in history . . . was a people so willing to fight and die with such a universal sense of duty. . . . We knew, and do not presume that we ignored it, that we would have been annihilated. . . . However, that didn't prompt us to ask you to withdraw the missiles, [and] that didn't prompt us to ask you to yield."[3]

Castro joined his people in working the sugarcane fields during harvest in April 1965.

on sugar. Unfortunately, his plan to diversify crop output failed. Farmers struggled with unfamiliar plants that did not readily thrive in Cuban soil. Islanders were forced to ration goods in order to survive the disaster.

Cuba struggled agriculturally and economically because of Castro's farming change. Castro worked to rectify the situation. He gained economic

assistance from the Soviet Union after a visit to
Moscow, Russia, in April 1963. He returned
agricultural emphasis to sugarcane by 1964.
Unhappy Cubans continued to flock to Miami.
From their perspective, time had revealed Castro's
promises to be little more than misguided fantasies
of a communist tyrant.

YEARS OF UNEASE AND ECONOMIC ADVERSITY

Castro referred to the numerous exiles who fled
the island as "worms" and "scum," but the United
States welcomed its new guests.[4] In 1966, the nation's
Cuban Refugee Act enabled more than 400,000
Cubans to enter the United States. Planes and boats
transported the steady stream of Cubans looking to
rebuild their lives in U.S. cities. Despite this exodus,
Castro maintained countless loyal followers. Many
of them wholeheartedly supported his mounting
guerrilla efforts to spread the communist revolution
internationally.

"We say and we declare that Cuban fighters can
be counted on by the revolutionary movement in any
corner of the earth," Castro promised.[5] Much to the
dissatisfaction of the United States and the Soviet
Union, these words were reinforced by the various

rebellions Castro urged throughout Latin America and Africa. The superpowers were still struggling for control across the globe, and Castro's latest interference benefited neither nation.

Nearly eight years after returning to Havana as Cuba's savior, Castro had lost some of his most trusted fighters, including Guevara. He had also lost the faith of a portion of his people. The economy was floundering, and his government was struggling to win enthusiasm for the communist ideal of not regarding labor as a means of achieving individual profit. Citizens who failed to conform to Castro's policies were faced with choosing between emigrating, shifting their attitudes, or risking imprisonment or harassment.

Even islanders who adored Castro struggled. By 1968, the Soviets had reduced their oil supply to Cuba,

No Loafing

In March 1971, Castro took measures that forced his people to adopt an improved work ethic. Part of the challenge he faced in enforcing communist economic policies was motivating laborers. Numerous workers were not inclined to push themselves or to even show up at their jobs merely to share a collective profit with the entire community.

To combat this dilemma, the Cuban government instituted an anti-loafing law that promised to punish laborers who demonstrated less than total commitment. Men and women who were frequently absent or deemed lazy faced consequences ranging from verbal warnings to sentences at detention centers. Castro was determined to make his people regard a rigorous work routine as a national responsibility rather than a personal goal.

and residents were ordered to ration their fuel. They were also forced to ration certain foods as a result of the ongoing U.S. embargo. Castro's thoughts on economic recovery offered little reassurance to Cubans. Under his communist influence, private businesses were confiscated and replaced with state-run institutions. Cubans were forced to abandon their old existences in favor of whatever new measures Castro was intent on putting into practice. For many, the transition was intolerable.

CASTRO'S CONTINUED LEADERSHIP

Sensing that his country was lapsing into crisis, Castro endorsed a somewhat dramatic economic strategy on July 26, 1969. The entire island would mobilize to yield a sugar crop so massive that it was certain to boost Cuba's desperate financial situation. People from all walks of life were to aid in agricultural efforts that he claimed would result in 10 million tons (9 million t) of the nation's chief export. Castro also took to the fields. He was certain that money from the crop would pay Cuba's debts.

The massive undertaking produced widespread disappointment. Castro announced on May 19, 1970, that Cuba was 15 percent short of its goal.

He suggested that perhaps the moment had come to resign. Citizens protested. Regardless of the turmoil of the past decade, Castro managed to captivate a sufficient percentage of Cubans still in Cuba. Despite starting the 1970s with the frustration of the sugarcane harvest, the years ahead appeared to be filled with promise.

In September 1971, Castro joined the Non-Aligned Movement, a collection of countries opposed to or independent from global superpowers. By July 1972, Cuba became a member of the Council for Mutual Economic Assistance, an organization formed by the Soviet Union to further trade

No Longer Allowed to Dream

Castro never wanted to appear as obviously restrictive of the press and freedom of speech as Batista. Still, he remained largely intolerant of any language or content that he believed opposed revolutionary ideals. Cuban poet Herberto Padilla learned this when he was imprisoned during the spring of 1971. The author had initially voiced great enthusiasm for Castro's revolution. With time, he had come to resent the loss of personal independence and self-expression that the communist regime ultimately imposed.

Padilla bitterly remarked in his work, "Cuban poets no longer dream (Not even at night). . . . Hands seize them by the shoulders/Turn them about."[6] His words revealed his disdain for Castro's secret police and oppression of individual opinion. They also invited Castro's wrath. Padilla was taken into custody. He was released about a month later on the condition that he must apologize publicly for his treasonous attitude. Padilla moved to the United States in 1981 and remained there until his death in December 2000.

Cuban and Angolan soldiers are shown during a weapon practice session at a training center in Angola in February 1976.

relations between communist governments. Castro had learned that Cuba could not sustain his revolutionary principles without some degree of outside assistance. Such collaborations soon led to a gradual upswing in his country's economy.

The United States briefly exhibited signs of warming to its southern neighbor. U.S. and Cuban officials had begun discussions about ending the embargo and reconciling. In 1975, President Gerald Ford temporarily suspended some of the U.S. trade restrictions against Cuba. But when Jimmy Carter took office as president in 1977, he was unwilling to ease restrictions on Cuba. Carter objected to the presence of Castro's troops in Angola, a nation in southwestern Africa. Various revolutionary groups in Angola were warring for independence from Portugal, which held Angola as a colony. Carter took a hard line and warned Castro that the leader's human rights violations on his island and refusal to leave Angola would block a renewed friendship with the United States. Castro refused to back down and insisted that the United States had no right to dictate where he could dispatch soldiers, saying, "What moral basis can a country have . . . whose troops are stationed right here on our own national territory."[7]

Although he would not relent in his negotiations with U.S. leaders, Castro tried to give the impression of

Angola

As Angolans struggled to free their country from centuries of Portuguese rule, three distinct groups formed to overthrow colonial authority. Castro sent military and political aid to a communist faction known as the Movimento Popular de Libertação de Angola (MPLA), or Popular Movement for the Liberation of Angola.

By October 1975, approximately 1,500 Cuban troops and more than 200 Cuban advisors were in Angola. When Portugal finally agreed to relinquish control of Angola in November, civil war erupted between parties seeking to control the new government. Due to Soviet and Cuban influence, the MPLA emerged victorious by early 1976. Skirmishes for power have continued into the twenty-first century.

being more accommodating with his own people. In 1976, a new constitution provided for the creation of a Cuban National Assembly. This legislative body was supposedly formed to represent the will of Cuban citizens through democratic processes such as voting and elections. However, this body's responsibilities were mainly to help with local improvements and problems, such as roads, housing, and bus schedules. In reality, the Communist Party remained the only political group permitted to have any true power in Cuba.

Castro ran for president of the National Assembly's State Council. No one was foolish enough to run against him and risk the consequences. Victorious, Castro continued to exercise almost absolute control in Cuba.

Castro was a strong, confident leader who never wavered in his belief
that he knew what was best for his country.

*Cuban refugees on a boat at the port of Mariel, Cuba,
wait to go to Florida in April 1980.*

The End of a
Superpower

Although no Cubans went without
food or the opportunity to work, the
1970s saw a large number of islanders disappointed
in their leader. Many were convinced Castro had
failed to provide the liberties he had promised upon

overthrowing Batista. Others were unsupportive of Castro's communist policies. These men and women were eager for a better life.

On April 1, 1980, six disenchanted citizens crashed a bus through the gates of the Peruvian Embassy in Havana. This dramatic dash for asylum resulted in gunfire and the death of a guard. It also triggered a tidal wave of approximately 10,000 like-minded refugees who crowded embassy grounds in the days that followed.

Castro was irate about this extremely public display of resistance to his authority. He dismissed the group as social misfits who could not withstand the righteous nature of his regime. He believed Cuba was better off without such citizens. On April 21, 1980, Castro declared that any Cubans who wanted to leave the island could do so through Mariel port. Exiles in the United States excitedly planned to send their own boats from Miami to Mariel port to retrieve their loved ones. President Jimmy Carter promised that Cuban

Castro's Family Life

Although Castro's life has inarguably been consumed by politics, he has managed to find time for family. In addition to his son Fidelito with Mirta Díaz-Balart in 1949, he has a daughter, Alina Fernández, with former mistress Natalia "Nati" Revuelta. Castro married Dalia Soto del Valle in 1980, though the couple had children long before they wed. The pair had five sons during the 1960s and 1970s: Alexis, Alexander, Alejandro, Antonio, and Angel.

immigrants would be welcomed. Carter initially said that the United States would accept 3,500 refugees and encouraged Latin American countries to welcome equal numbers. However, there was a massive influx of Cubans into the United States.

Carter could not have imagined how open U.S. citizens would have to be to accommodate the sudden and expansive influx. During the next few months, approximately 125,000 Cubans flooded the United States. This spurred tensions with their new U.S. neighbors. Exiles stretched housing and employment resources, and many were unwilling to blend into U.S. culture. This was especially so for the sizable percentage of Cubans who hoped to return to Cuba once Castro was no longer in power. It made no sense to these immigrants to completely forsake their roots in exchange for refuge.

The frustrations of many U.S. citizens increased when they discovered that tens of thousands

Challenging Voyage

Although the Cubans who participated in the Mariel Boatlift were sailing toward freedom, their journey was not always jubilant. Overcrowded, battered vessels and rough Atlantic waters made capsized crafts a regular reality. Twenty-seven Cubans died during transport. In addition, the U.S. Coast Guard issued more than 1,200 boating safety violations and spent approximately $650,000 each week during the boat lift.

of Cuban immigrants had criminal backgrounds or psychiatric problems. Castro had freed scores of prisoners and mental-ward residents, so that they could join the exodus. He wanted to prove that the exiles represented the undesirables who polluted his country. Regardless of which leader appeared the most foolish, the Mariel Boatlift, as it had become known, ended in October 1980.

The End of an Era

When President Ronald Reagan was sworn into office in January 1981, it seemed that Cuba would be up against another Kennedy. Reagan made it quite clear that he was dedicated to combating communism. He boosted military spending and began conducting naval maneuvers in the Caribbean Sea. Reagan did not hesitate to express his distaste for Castro or his willingness to do whatever was necessary to protect U.S. interests and take a stand against Cuba's oppressive government.

Tensions reached a boiling point in October 1983. Cuban and Soviet forces were constructing an international airport in Grenada, an island in the southeastern Caribbean. Reagan suggested the activity was more of a military threat than an effort

U.S. soldiers in Grenada, November 2, 1983

to boost tourism. Fearing the spread of communism so close to U.S. soil, Reagan was quick to invade Grenada when bloody political unrest rocked the island. Nearly 9,000 U.S. soldiers landed on Grenada on October 26, 1983. They captured 642 Cubans and killed 24. The United States was successful. Reagan was overjoyed. Castro was furious. More troubling developments were in store for Cuba and its leader.

For years, Cuba depended on support from the Soviet Union. The communist superpower had long purchased the sugar and other island exports that the United States refused to buy. The Soviets also supplied Cubans with oil and other essential products. Moreover, the Soviet Union formed the backbone of the economic and political policies that Castro believed in and imposed on his people. It came as a devastating blow when new Soviet Premier Mikhail Gorbachev indicated that it was time for rigid communist principles to change.

The United States had steadily been winning the upper hand in the military and technological advances that shaped the Cold War. As competition between the superpowers cooled, Reagan and Gorbachev forged closer relations during the late 1980s. The world sensed Gorbachev's push toward democracy. Castro reacted by firmly upholding the strict communist ideologies that defined his revolution.

Cuba Will Not Stray

Although he was undoubtedly alarmed by Gorbachev's willingness to stray from the rigid communist policies that had previously defined the Soviet Union, Castro was determined that Cuba would not follow in Eastern Europe's footsteps. "Nothing and nobody will make our fatherland turn back from the socialist path," he proclaimed during a speech on January 1, 1990.[1] Even as Soviet communism began to crumble in the months ahead, Castro never wavered. He continued to rally the people with remarks such as "Socialism or death, fatherland or death, we will win!"[2]

The Soviet Union formally dissolved in
December 1991 and gave way to several individual
Eastern European governments. The Cold War had
ended. Castro lost a powerful ally and approximately
$6 billion in annual aid.

UN Reaction

Cuba has been a United Nations (UN) member since October 24, 1945. Castro's interactions with the UN have always been somewhat volatile. UN officials have criticized policies they believe jeopardize islanders' basic liberties and attacked foreign embargoes that injure Cuba's finances.

Dedicated to promoting international peace, security, and economic progress, the UN unflinchingly took Castro to task in February 1989. At that time, the organization published a 400-page report detailing how Cubans were routinely deprived of the freedom of speech and the right to assemble. Specifically, the report explained how residents were denied the ability to express unpopular political opinions without risking torture or unjust imprisonment.

During the 1990s, the UN repeatedly addressed U.S. trade restrictions against Cuba. A majority of delegates argued that U.S. actions ultimately had a much more devastating effect on average Cuban citizens than Castro. By 1999, UN representatives voted approximately eight times against the U.S. decision to maintain its embargo against Cuba.

NEW HEADLINES IN AN ONGOING CONFLICT

During the early 1990s, U.S. officials and exiles alike predicted Castro's downfall. Many believed he could not possibly withstand the mounting unpopularity and economic struggles. The number of exiles exploded once more. In response, the United States set a limit in 1994 to 20,000 Cuban immigrants per year. Despite this policy, scores of Cubans kept making risky sea crossings.

In February 1996, four exiles piloted fighter planes over international waters during a search for refugees in need of assistance. Castro's military fired at the aircraft, which belonged to the Miami-based group Brothers to the Rescue. All four men were killed. The move triggered heightened criticism from the U.S. government, which answered the bloodshed by maintaining its embargo. Much of the global community objected to these trade restrictions, noting that they wounded the Cuban people more than Castro. Famous figures, including Pope John Paul II and Jimmy Carter, expressed that there had to be a way to restore individual freedoms without cutting off Cuba's economic lifeline.

Debate surrounding the embargo was not the only reason Cuba's interactions with the United States

The Pope's Visit

When Pope John Paul II visited Cuba in January 1998, adoring crowds in Havana celebrated the religious leader's condemnation of the U.S. embargo. They also voiced their enthusiasm for the pontiff's plea that individual liberties and improved human rights be restored to the Cuban people. He pointedly reminded listeners, "Suffering is not only physical. . . . There is also suffering of the soul, such as we see in those who are isolated, persecuted, [or] imprisoned for various offenses or for reasons of conscience, for ideas which, though dissident [unpopular], are nonetheless peaceful."[3]

attracted worldwide attention. On November 25, 1999, five-year-old Elián González was found floating in an inner tube approximately 3 miles (4.8 km) from the Florida coast. He and 12 other refugees had fled Cuba for the United States. All of the other passengers had perished during the crossing, including Elián's mother.

Elián's parents were divorced. Elián's father, Juan Miguel González, was not aware of his ex-wife's plans to go to the United States. As soon as González learned of his son's situation, he demanded that Elián be immediately returned to Havana. Relatives in Miami—as well as that city's massive Cuban population—welcomed the youngster. They also vowed that Elián would never again set foot on the island his mother had died trying to escape. Castro and his followers quickly put their support behind González as he fought to be reunited with his son. It was not certain where this young boy would fit into the whirlwind of conflict between the United States and Cuba. ⌐

Five-year-old Elián González became caught in a political tug-of-war between Cuba and the United States.

Fidel Castro gives a speech in Havana, Cuba, in September 2002.

CUBA IN THE TWENTY-FIRST CENTURY

As the months passed, it became increasingly obvious that Elián's predicament was far from a simple custody case. The question of whether he would begin a new life with the exiles in Florida or return to his homeland demonstrated the conflicting emotions that tore apart Cubans in both countries. U.S. citizens were also divided on the issue. Some believed the boy had made great sacrifices to come to their country and, therefore, was entitled to all the freedoms it offers. Others accused Elián's supporters in Miami of being unwilling to adapt to U.S. laws. They argued that it was his relatives' duty to comply with the government when U.S. Immigration and Naturalization Services demanded that the boy be sent back to Cuba in January 2000.

After court battles and intense controversy, U.S. Attorney General Janet Reno announced in April that Elián was to be returned to Cuba to be raised by his father. On April 24, 2000, heavily armed federal agents seized the child from the house where he had been residing in Miami. Elián arrived in Havana on June 28.

As tensions calmed following the dramatic events surrounding Elián, Cuba remained at the forefront of international affairs. The United States felt pressure from the United Nations (UN) and several of its

No U.S. Currency

Although Castro's government has periodically permitted use of the U.S. dollar to stimulate the economy, the currency was officially banned in November 2004. This action was intended to fight back against what Cuban officials perceived as the continuation of harsh U.S. trade restrictions, such as the embargo.

member states to repeal the embargo
that continued to cripple Cuba's
economy. The world would not
forget or ignore Castro's role in the
Cold War, the masses of unhappy
islanders who had fled his authority,
and his ongoing dedication to a
strict communist system. Yet, many
Cubans and U.S. citizens could
not help but question whether
the moment was right for the two
countries to reconcile.

U.S. Relations

By the dawn of the new
millennium, it appeared that some
strides were being made toward more
friendly relations between Cuba
and the United States. Namely, the
Trade Sanctions Reform and Export
Enhancement Act of 2000 permits
U.S. companies to sell food and
agricultural products to Cuba for
cash. While U.S. businesses are not
allowed to obtain Cuban goods for

Guantánamo Bay

Despite ongoing tensions
between Cuba and the
United States, U.S. offi-
cials continue to maintain
their naval base at Guan-
tánamo Bay. According
to the U.S. Navy, "It is the
oldest U.S. naval station
outside the continental
[United States] and the
only one in a country that
does not enjoy an open
political relationship with
the United States."[1]

Castro's government
regards such a foreign
military presence as ille-
gal. The outpost is critical
to U.S. interests in the Caribbean. It has also been
used as a detention camp
for men and women sus-
pected of plotting terrorist
acts against the United
States, especially since
the attack on September
11, 2001.

sale in the United States—and though the embargo has never been lifted officially—the act prompted a major economic shift. In 2006, Cubans bought approximately $328 million in goods from U.S. distributors. Rice, wheat, poultry, corn, and soybeans constitute the bulk of items U.S. businesses provide to their Cuban clients.

Progress seemed to extend beyond trade agreements. In 2001, island officials discussed repaying Cuban-Americans for losses they sustained when their property was seized during the revolution four decades earlier. The offer was ultimately rejected, but a greater number of U.S. government representatives began to tour Cuba and acknowledge its accomplishments in education and health care.

Jimmy Carter, the former U.S. president who had been criticized for the part he played in the Mariel Boatlift, visited Cuba in May 2002 and met with Castro. He also addressed Cubans in a televised

Cuba's Superior Students

In 2001, the United Nations Education, Scientific, and Cultural Organization (UNESCO) reported that Cuba's elementary students achieved test scores and demonstrated literacy levels superior to what was observed in the rest of Latin America. "Cuba far and away led the region in third- and fourth-grade mathematics and language achievement," noted a member of the UNESCO panel. "Even the lowest fourth of Cuban students performed above the regional average."[2]

speech that stressed his disagreement with the U.S. embargo and urged them to consider political change. Carter concluded by saying:

> *After forty-three years of animosity, we hope that someday soon, you can reach across the great divide that separates our two countries and say, "We are ready to join the community of democracies." And I hope that the people of the United States will soon open their arms to you and say, "We welcome you as friends."[3]*

In contrast to Carter, President George W. Bush has demonstrated his support for a continuation of the embargo. He has also increased restrictions on tourism to Cuba. In addition, the ongoing threat of terrorism within the global community has left some U.S. officials cautiously contemplating what potential risk Castro's regime might pose. Although he condemned the attacks of September 11, 2001, Castro has visited nations such as Iran, Libya, and Syria. The United States has experienced hostilities with each of these countries. As of 2007, the U.S. Department of State continues to recognize the 1982 U.S. designation of Cuba as a nation that has "repeatedly provided support for international acts of terrorism."[4]

Fidel and Raúl Castro in March 2003

CONFLICTING LEGACIES

Regardless of how many U.S. leaders might have preferred to see Castro removed from office, Cuba's National Assembly extended his presidency by another five years in 2003. By that point, however, rumors were swirling about the 76-year-old's health. In recent years, the press has theorized that Castro suffers from ailments ranging from cancer to Parkinson's disease. On July 31, 2006, Castro fueled discussion of his mounting frailty after transferring power to brother Raúl in order to recover from a surgery to correct intestinal problems.

Cuban officials emphasized that this transition was only temporary and that their beloved head of state would eventually resume full responsibilities. On February 19, 2008, however, Castro officially resigned from the presidency. After nearly a half-century in power, he was the world's longest-serving national leader. In a letter to his people, Castro wrote:

> *I always exercised the necessary prerogatives to carry forward our revolutionary work with the support of the vast majority of the people. . . . My desire was always to carry out my duties until my final breath. That is what I have to offer. . . . The path will always be difficult and will require the intelligent strength of all of us. . . . Always prepare for the worst scenario. "Be as prudent in success as you stand firm in adversity" is a principle that must not be forgotten. The adversary we must defeat is extremely strong, but we have kept him at bay for half a century. . . . I do not bid you farewell. My only wish is to fight as a soldier of ideas.[5]*

Castro's decision concluded nearly 50 years of his unquestionable—and unforgettable—control of his beloved island.

On February 24, 2008, Raúl Castro was officially named president of Cuba following unanimous selection by the National Assembly. It is too soon to tell how this change in command will affect Cuba. In response to the change in leadership, U.S. Assistant Secretary of State Tom Shannon said, "There is a possibility and potential for change in Cuba, but those changes will have to be born inside Cuba."[6]

Time will ultimately reveal whether Fidel Castro's revolution will survive his absence. What is unarguable is that the effect of his

Reaction to Castro's Resignation

U.S. President George W. Bush: "The U.S. will help the people of Cuba realize the blessings of liberty."

Venezuelan President Hugo Chavez: "Fidel is not giving up or abandoning anything—he is occupying the post that he has to fill in the Cuban revolution and the Latin American revolution. . . . Men like Fidel never retire."

Gordon Brown, the British prime minister: "We can only hope that a new path will open up after this withdrawal and that there will be more democracy in that country."

Swedish Foreign Minister Carl Bildt: "The withdrawal of Fidel Castro marks the end of an era that began with high hopes but ended with oppression."

French Minister of State Jean-Pierre Jouyet: "One cannot but hope that after this retirement a new path will open and that there will be democracy."

Russian Communist Party Chief Gennady Zyuganov: "It is a courageous decision, and in taking it, Fidel Castro, I am sure, was guided by the interests of his country and his people."[7]

death, when it comes, will resound
worldwide. The international
implications could spur an immense
homeward wave of exiles, create a tide
of violent local unrest, or facilitate
renewed relations with the United
States.

Castro's memory will undeniably
be cherished by those Cubans who
have benefited from his socialist
reforms. It will also forever be
despised by the throngs of Cubans
who fled the more repressive aspects
of his government. Castro will
undoubtedly be recalled with both resentment and
begrudging respect by leaders who witnessed his
bold guerrilla rebellion and his belligerence during
the Cuban Missile Crisis. Regardless of how anyone
evaluates Fidel Castro, it is clear that the man who
has come to symbolize Cuba is completely confident
in the course his life has followed and the effect he
has had on his country. ⌐

After Castro's nearly half century as ruler of Cuba, his influence on the country and the world is undeniable.

TIMELINE

1926

Fidel Alejandro Castro Ruz is born on August 13 in Cuba.

1933–1945

Castro attends school at La Salle College, Dolores College, and Belén College.

1945–1950

Castro studies law and social science at Havana University. He devotes most of his time to political activism.

1957

In January, Castro and his army initiate attacks on military garrisons and isolated Cuban troops in the Sierra Maestra.

1959

Batista flees Cuba on January 1. Castro becomes prime minister on February 16.

1959

On May 17, Castro creates laws that force plantation owners to give up their land, which is given to the underclass.

1952

Fulgencio Batista stages a coup and becomes dictator of Cuba on March 10.

1953

Castro is taken prisoner on August 1 and tried for fighting Batista. He is sentenced to 15 years in prison.

1955

On May 6, Castro is released from prison early.

1960

In February, Castro and Soviet Premier Khrushchev develop a controversial trade agreement.

1960

U.S. officials increase trade restrictions with Cuba in the summer.

1961

U.S. diplomatic relations are severed with Cuba in January.

1961

The Bay of Pigs invasion on April 17 by U.S.-trained Cuban exiles fails to overthrow Castro's regime.

1962

President John F. Kennedy authorizes a trade embargo on Cuba in February.

1962

In July, Castro agrees to allow the Soviets to place medium-range nuclear missiles in Cuba.

1967

In October, Che Guevara is executed for waging guerrilla unrest in Bolivia as part of Castro's efforts to spread communism in Latin America.

1980

The Mariel Boatlift begins in April. As many as 125,000 Cubans move to the United States.

1981

U.S. soldiers invade Grenada on October 26, capturing 642 Cubans and killing 24.

1962

In mid-October, the Cuban Missile Crisis results in a U.S.-Soviet fight over Cuba.

1962

On October 28, the United States and the Soviet Union announce an end to the Cuban Missile Crisis.

1966

In 1966, the Cuban Refugee Act enables more than 400,000 islanders to enter the United States.

1991

The Soviet Union officially dissolves in December, and Castro loses as much as $6 billion in annual aid.

2006

On July 31, Castro transfers power to his brother Raúl in order to recover from surgery.

2008

On February 19, Fidel Castro resigns as Cuba's leader. Raúl Castro is named president on February 24.

ESSENTIAL FACTS

DATE OF BIRTH

August 13, 1926

PLACE OF BIRTH

Cuba

PARENTS

Ángel Castro and Lina Ruz González

EDUCATION

La Salle College, Dolores College, Belén College, Havana University

MARRIAGE

❖ Mirta Díaz-Balart, 1948
❖ Dalia Soto del Valle, 1980

CHILDREN

❖ With Mirta Díaz-Balart: Felix Fidel, or "Fidelito"
❖ With Natalia Revuelta: Alina Fernández
❖ With Dalia Soto del Valle: Alexis, Alexander, Alejandro, Antonio, and Angel

CAREER HIGHLIGHTS

Nearly a half century in power, Fidel Castro was the world's longest-serving national leader. After he and his guerrilla army defeated Batista, Cuba's abusive dictator, Castro was praised as a hero. He fought for the underclass in Cuba, striving to give all Cubans equal access to housing, education, health care, and employment. He became a controlling leader whose strong personality and beliefs garnered enemies and allies. Cubans were among the many people who were unhappy with Castro and his government. Some Cuban exiles who had settled in the United States attempted to overthrow Castro in the Bay of Pigs in April 1961, but failed. Other enemies included the United States, while allies included the Soviet Union. Castro's relationships with the two superpowers, as well as the strife already between the United States and the Soviet Union, brought the world to the edge of a nuclear war.

SOCIETAL CONTRIBUTION

Although his words and actions have been disliked by countless individuals and numerous national governments, Castro brought education, employment, and health care to Cubans least able to afford such necessities.

CONFLICTS

The strong-willed and determined leader fought with fellow citizens and other world leaders as he tried to uphold his beliefs in what was best for Cuba and strove to control the nation he loved.

QUOTE

"Sentence me. I don't mind. History will absolve me."
—*Fidel Castro, 1953*

ADDITIONAL RESOURCES

SELECT BIBLIOGRAPHY

Castro, Fidel. *Fidel Castro Speaks.* Ed. Martin Kenner and James Petras. New York: Grove Press Inc., 1969.

Castro, Fidel. *History Will Absolve Me.* Secaucus, NJ: Lyle Stuart Inc., 1984.

Castro, Fidel, and Frei Betto. *Fidel and Religion: Castro Talks on Revolution and Religion with Frei Betto.* New York: Simon and Schuster, 1987.

Elliot, Jeffrey M., and Mervyn M. Dymally. *Fidel Castro: Nothing Can Stop the Course of History.* New York: Pathfinder Press, 1986.

Skierka, Volker. *Fidel Castro: A Biography.* Trans. Patrick Camiller. Malden, MA: Polity Press, 2004.

FURTHER READING

January, Brendan. *Fidel Castro: Cuban Revolutionary.* New York: Franklin Watts, 2003.

Naden, Corinne J., and Rose Blue. *Fidel Castro and the Cuban Revolution.* Greensboro, NC: Morgan Reynolds Publishing, 2006.

Press, Petra. *Fidel Castro: An Unauthorized Biography.* Portsmouth, NH: Heinemann Library, 2000.

Web Links

To learn more about Fidel Castro, visit ABDO Publishing Company online at **www.abdopublishing.com**. Web sites about Fidel Castro are featured on our Book Links page. These links are routinely monitored and updated to provide the most current information available.

Places to Visit

Arizona State University Art Museum
51 East Tenth Street, Tempe, AZ 85281
480-965-2787
asuartmuseum.asu.edu/collections/lacat.htm
The museum's Latin American collection includes the biggest and most noteworthy works by Cuban artists of the 1990s.

Historical Museum of Southern Florida
101 West Flagler Street, Miami, FL 33130
305-375-1492
www.hmsf.org
The museum has collections about the cultures of South Florida and the Caribbean, including Caribbean areas that have influenced Florida history, such as Cuba.

Museum of Arts and Sciences: Cuban Foundation Museum
352 S. Nova Road, Daytona Beach, FL 32114
386-255-0285
www.moas.org/Cuban%20Art.html
The museum holds one of the most important collections of Cuban art outside of Cuba. The collection of more than 200 art objects documents three centuries of Cuban history.

Glossary

asylum
Refuge or shelter.

bond
A certificate of debt generally issued by a government or a business.

capitalism
An economic system that supports private ownership of industry and allows individuals to maximize personal profits.

Cold War
Political tensions that existed between the United States and the Soviet Union from about 1945 to 1990. The relationship was characterized by intense competition in areas ranging from space exploration to the production of military arms.

communism
A communal economic and political system that stresses workers should control production in a society. In a true communist state, social classes cease to exist, government is unnecessary, and everyone lives in abundance. Today, the term refers to authoritarian political systems whose leaders claim to advance the rights of the masses, peasants, and workers.

democracy
A government in which citizens rule by majority vote. The term *democracy* is derived from two Greek words: *demos* means "people" and *kratos* means "rule" or "power."

dictator
A ruler who exercises absolute control and authority in a manner that is often oppressive or abusive.

diplomatic
Related to formalized negotiations between nations.

embargo
The prohibition of commerce and trade with a certain country as a form of punishment.

emigrate
> To leave one country to reside in another.

garrison
> A military post.

guerrilla
> A soldier who belongs to an independent armed force that participates in irregular warfare rather than using tactics more common to organized, formal warfare.

ideologies
> Political ideas or visions.

immigrate
> To arrive in one country from another to take up residence.

mangrove
> A type of tropical tree or shrub that typically thrives in saltwater marshes.

nationalize
> To put under the authority or control of the state or government.

regime
> A government structure.

revolutionary
> An activist who aggressively attempts to bring about radical change, often to a government structure or a political system.

socialism
> A political ideology that supports government regulation of the economy to produce a more equitable distribution of wealth and well-being among citizens.

sugarcane
> A plant with strong, flexible stems that contain a juicy sap used as a source of molasses and commercial sugar.

SOURCE NOTES

Chapter 1. A Powerful Promise

1. Volker Skierka. *Fidel Castro: A Biography*. Trans. Patrick Camiller. Malden, MA: Polity Press, 2004. 47.

2. Leycester Coltman. *The Real Fidel Castro*. New Haven, CT: Yale University Press, 2003. 114.

3. "FACTBOX: Quotes from Fidel Castro." *Reuters.com*. 19 Feb. 2008. Thomson Reuters. 2 May 2008 <http://www.reuters.com/article/topNews/idUSN1922656120080219>.

4. Anthony DePalma. *The Man Who Invented Fidel: Castro, Cuba, and Herbert L. Matthews of the* New York Times. New York: PublicAffairs, 2006. 14.

5. Rufo López-Fresquet. *My Fourteen Months with Castro*. New York: The World Publishing Company, 1966. 186–187.

6. Ibid. 187.

7. Leycester Coltman. *The Real Fidel Castro*. New Haven, CT: Yale University Press, 2003. 112.

Chapter 2. Young Fidel

1. Volker Skierka. *Fidel Castro: A Biography*. Trans. Patrick Camiller. Malden, MA: Polity Press, 2004. 6.

2. Jeffrey M. Elliot and Mervyn M. Dymally. *Fidel Castro: Nothing Can Stop the Course of History*. New York: Pathfinder Press, 1986. 13.

3. Robert E. Quirk. *Fidel Castro*. New York: W. W. Norton & Company, 1993. 14.

4. Volker Skierka. *Fidel Castro: A Biography*. Trans. Patrick Camiller. Malden, MA: Polity Press, 2004. 11.

5. Fidel Castro and Frei Betto. *Fidel and Religion: Castro Talks on Revolution and Religion with Frei Betto*. New York: Simon and Schuster, 1987. 122.

6. Volker Skierka. *Fidel Castro: A Biography*. Trans. Patrick Camiller. Malden, MA: Polity Press, 2004. 14.

Chapter 3. Intent on Change

1. Volker Skierka. *Fidel Castro: A Biography*. Trans. Patrick Camiller. Malden, MA: Polity Press, 2004. 27.

2. Robert E. Quirk. *Fidel Castro*. New York: W. W. Norton & Company, 1993. 46.

3. Ibid.

4. Juan M. Clark. "Don't Fall for Castro's Charm." *Florida International University: Free Cuba Foundation* 3 Nov. 1998. 6 Oct. 2007 <http://www.fiu.edu/~fcf/castroscharmdontfall.html>.
5. Fidel Castro and Frei Betto. *Fidel and Religion: Castro Talks on Revolution and Religion with Frei Betto*. New York: Simon and Schuster, 1987. 152.
6. Ibid. 152.
7. Robert E. Quirk. *Fidel Castro*. New York: W. W. Norton & Company, 1993. 51.

Chapter 4. Prisoner, Exile, Leader
1. Fidel Castro. *History Will Absolve Me*. Secaucus, NJ: Lyle Stuart Inc., 1984. 120.
2. Volker Skierka. *Fidel Castro: A Biography*. Trans. Patrick Camiller. Malden, MA: Polity Press, 2004. 39.
3. Fidel Castro and Frei Betto. *Fidel and Religion: Castro Talks on Revolution and Religion with Frei Betto*. New York: Simon and Schuster, 1987. 168.
4. Fidel Castro. *History Will Absolve Me*. Secaucus, NJ: Lyle Stuart Inc., 1984. 50–51.
5. Fidel Castro. *Fidel Castro Speaks*. Ed. Martin Kenner and James Petras. New York: Grove Press, Inc., 1969. 181–184.
6. Fidel Castro and Frei Betto. *Fidel and Religion: Castro Talks on Revolution and Religion with Frei Betto*. New York: Simon and Schuster, 1987. 165–166.

Chapter 5. ¡Viva Fidel!
1. Robert E. Quirk. *Fidel Castro*. New York: W. W. Norton & Company, 1993. 189.
2. Anthony DePalma. *The Man Who Invented Fidel: Castro, Cuba, and Herbert L. Matthews of the New York Times*. New York: PublicAffairs, 2006. 91.
3. Ibid. 92.
4. Ibid. 97–98.
5. Robert E. Quirk. *Fidel Castro*. New York: W. W. Norton & Company, 1993. 219.
6. Ibid. 222.
7. Karl Marx and Friedrich Engels. *The Communist Manifesto*. Trans. Samuel Moore. London: Penguin Group, 2002. 180.
8. Volker Skierka. *Fidel Castro: A Biography*. Trans. Patrick Camiller. Malden, MA: Polity Press, 2004. 68.

Source Notes Continued

Chapter 6. Maximum Leader

1. Robert E. Quirk. *Fidel Castro*. New York: W. W. Norton & Company, 1993. 228.
2. Ibid. 251.
3. Fidel Castro. "On the Promulgation of the Agrarian Law." 17 May 1959. *Latin American Network Information Center*, University of Texas at Austin. 14 Oct. 2007 <http://lanic.utexas.edu/la/cb/cuba/castro/1959/19590517>.
4. Volker Skierka. *Fidel Castro: A Biography*. Trans. Patrick Camiller. Malden, MA: Polity Press, 2004. 99.
5. John F. Kennedy. Speech at Democratic Dinner. Cincinnati, OH, 6 Oct. 1960. *The American Presidency Project*, University of California at Santa Barbara. 3 May 2008 <http://www.presidency.ucsb.edu/ws/index.php?pid=25660>.
6. Robert E. Quirk. *Fidel Castro*. New York: W. W. Norton & Company, 1993. 321.
7. Fidel Castro. Broadcast interview. 23 Oct. 1962 *Latin American Network Information Center*, University of Texas at Austin. 3 May 2008 <http://lanic.utexas.edu/la/cb/cuba/castro/1962/19621024>.

Chapter 7. Struggling to Survive

1. Robert E. Quirk. *Fidel Castro*. New York: W. W. Norton & Company, 1993. 448.
2. Ibid.
3. James G. Blight and Janet M. Lang. *The Fog of War: Lessons from the Life of Robert S. McNamara*. Lanham, MD: Rowman & Littlefield, 2005. 72.
4. "Tremors in Cuba Bending Exiles' Hard Line." *NYTimes.com*. 6 Oct. 1993. 3 May 2008 <http://query.nytimes.com/gst/fullpage.html?res=9F0CE6DB1231F935A35753C1A965958260&sec=&spon=&pagewanted=print>.
5. Fidel Castro. "Tricontinental Conference." 16 Jan. 1966. *Latin American Network Information Center*, University of Texas at Austin. 3 May 2008 <http://lanic.utexas.edu/la/cb/cuba/castro/1966/19660216>.
6. Volker Skierka. *Fidel Castro: A Biography*. Trans. Patrick Camiller. Malden, MA: Polity Press, 2004. 214.
7. Ibid. 210.

Chapter 8. The End of a Superpower

1. Fidel Castro. "Castro Salutes People on Revolution Anniversary." 1 Jan. 1990. *Latin American Network Information Center*, University of Texas at Austin. 3 May 2008 <http://www1.lanic.utexas.edu/la/cb/cuba/castro/1990/19900101.1>.

2. Fidel Castro. "Castro Speaks on Country's Current Problems." 5 June 1990. *Latin American Network Information*, University of Texas at Austin. 3 May 2008 <http://www1.lanic.utexas.edu/la/cb/cuba/castro/1990/19900605>.

3. "Pope Advocates Peace, Freedom in Final Mass." *CNN.com*. 25 Jan. 1998. 3 May 2008 <http://www.cnn.com/WORLD/9801/25/pope.mass/index.html>.

Chapter 9. Cuba in the Twenty-first Century

1. "About U.S. Naval Station Guantánamo Bay, Cuba." *U.S. Navy*. 3 May 2008 <http://www.cnic.navy.mil/Guantanamo/AboutGTMO/index.htm>.

2. Christopher Marquis. "Cuba Leads Latin America in Primary Education, Study Finds." *NYTimes.com*. 14 Dec. 2001. 3 May 2008 <http://query.nytimes.com/gst/fullpage.html?res=FF937A25751C1A9679C8B63>.9405EFDC103>.

3. Carter Gonzalez. "Carter Addresses the Cuban Nation and Urges Reform." *NYTimes.com*. 15 May 2002. 3 May 2008 <http://query.nytimes.com/gst/fullpage.html?res=9B01E0DB1339F936A25756C0A9649C8B63&sec=&spon=&pagewanted=print>.

4. "State Sponsors of Terrorism." *State.gov*. 23 Oct. 2007. 3 May 2008 <http://www.state.gov/s/ct/c14151.htm>.

5. "Excerpts from Castro's letter." *BBCNews.com*. 19 Feb. 2008. 29 Feb. 2008 <http://news.bbc.co.uk/2/hi/americas/7252236.stm>.

6. "Raul Castro named Cuban president." *BBCNews.com*. 25 Feb. 2008. 29 Feb. 2008 <http://news.bbc.co.uk/2/hi/americas/7261204.stm>.

7. "Reaction as Fidel Castro retires." *BBCNews.com*. 25 Feb. 2008. 29 Feb. 2008 <http://news.bbc.co.uk/2/hi/americas/7252306.stm>.

8. Caren Bohan. "Bush Calls Castro Government a 'Dying Order.'" *Reuters.com*. 24 Oct. 2007 3 May 2008 <http://www.reuters.com/article/politicsNews/idUSN2447794620071025>.

Index

ABOUT THE AUTHOR

Katie Marsico writes children's books from her home near Chicago, Illinois. She lives with her husband, Carl, and their two children, Maria and C. J. Before beginning her career as an author, Ms. Marsico worked as a managing editor in children's publishing.

PHOTO CREDITS